Sets In The West

A Collection of Poems

by

Ryan Fredric Steinbeck

Copyright © 2014 by Ryan Fredric Steinbeck

ISBN: 978-0-578-14973-8

Printed in the United States of America.

First Printing

www.ryanfsteinbeck.com

For further information about Ryan Fredric Steinbeck titles please visit the website above.

ryan@ryanfsteinbeck.com

LEGAL NOTICE.

All rights reserved. No part of this book may be used, reproduced, stored in a retrieval system, or transmitted in any form or manner whatsoever by any means: electronic, photocopying, mechanical, or otherwise, without written permission except in the case of brief quotations embodied in critical articles and reviews.

Requests to publish work from this book must be sent to Ryan Fredric Steinbeck

Acknowledgements

Thanks to my friends and family who have supported me and whose experiences have built and inspired many aspects of the characters in this book. Thank you to the artists who continue to inspire and challenge me.

Thanks to Cindy for the photos, and for tolerating and humoring the person that I am.

Thanks to Michael Steinbeck for the selflessness, patience, and again, the covers. I asked a lot of you this year.

To the Reader

I was going to avoid using this title for a collection. To me, it felt too obvious after *Rises In The East,* and I don't like obvious. However, weeks of second guessing did not provide anything more appropriate. Considering this collection wasn't planned, I realized there wasn't a more appropriate title to sum up the darker topics of death and coping, as well as soul and identity searching. Losing loved ones makes for a challenging year emotionally and I was essentially forced by my own subconscious to complete this collection before I could move on. Looking back, I understand it was its own therapy, both for me and for the characters in this book, who, in the end, begin to find their way out of the dark. My hope is to provide some resolve to any reader who has experienced similar situations.

Thank you for your support.

Table of Contents:

Sets in the West	1
Red Sun and Apocalyptic Sky	2
Dimming Lights	3
Electricity	4
Healing Light	5
Brook	6
Apparitions of Consequence	7
First Day	8
Modified Journey	9
If I Live to See Tomorrow	10
Days Later	11
The Water Comes to Meet You	12
Memories and Photographs	13
Empty Chair	14
Light on the Floor	15
Zone of Exclusion	16
Seventeen Years	17
I Remember	18
How Long	19
Tide	20
Intersect	21
Life Flashes	22
Broken Moon	23
The Walk Alone	24-25
Gift	26
These Hands	27
For the First Time in a Long Time	28
The Private Time After	29
Until We Live	30
Adhesive	31
Rules	32
Fortune Teller	33
Different Roads	34

Table of Contents:

Conversation with a Ghost in a Bar	35-36
Quiet Time	37
Winter's Tampering	38
Seeds of Optimism	39
Dear Ambivalence	40
Shallow	41
Remembering a Friend	42
Apology	43
Largest of Misconceptions	44
Surge Inside	45
The Day When Nothing Happens	46
One of Those Stories	47
One Eternal Moment	48
Revelations in a Pub	49
Transparent Reflection	50
Core Sample	51
Trespass	52
These Wings	53
Where I End	54

For Ricky

Sets in the West

My conscience roamed desolate darkness
in search of your acquaintance
Unsure if I deserved what I had

Sifting through my head
scattered in elemental layers
there was a Morse code message
I should've predicted
The afternoon understood
what the morning couldn't predict

I read fables of a rising
emerging in the east
They claimed inevitability
had dispersed through dimensions
as all that was real had slipped away

I gave you to the mountain sky
released you over water
In tumbling lake effect snow you were free

Clouds molded over us in arcs
Conforming to impervious north winds
A great companion lit my lithosphere
My eyes have been forced to adjust

As it set in the west
transient dark birds turned northward
What goes up must come down
Without a curtain call
you were silently written out of my play

Always to be a legend in my heart
Goodbye old friend

Red Sun and Apocalyptic Sky

We find our sweet spot
set down the blanket and picnic basket
prepare ourselves for the aging
Inching toward the time
when there will be no time at all
I sense a source of heat
but I've gone cold
The red sun is setting
beyond the bitter sea

I'm thankful you're here with me
for the party at the end of the world
Eyes on metallic grey skies
rusting into beauty
giving way to bombs a flare

There's a call to arms
a means of exaggeration
a soul under siege
as it searches for peace

Absolve the mind of mirage
Forgive ourselves on this fragmented beach
Another opportunity escapes our reach

Dimming Lights

We shined long ago
Burned too hot
Now dimming lights
We pulled the plug on each other
never appreciating technology that much

It grew problematic
Trace our wires and sparks
to a single night
when decisions were made for us
after which it went dark
We malfunctioned
When repaired we shone in opposite directions

At the end of the street
are the mirrors of regret
Reflections behind us
I glimpse your face
reminisce about abandoned rails and roads
I can't decide which path is the mistake
The one illuminated before me today
or the one I didn't take

Electricity

A final argument
The auroral display
Beautiful luminescence
before the fall of empires

Enumeration
Recalculation
No longer matching the visions in our heads

The ground is stable but useless
On the surface of us we are figments
We called what we had ability
It was hardly an equivalent
with nothing to command or control
no buttons to push for restart

The remedies we could've used
the things we could've said
swarm us like insects
as we light vigil candles
to mourn the loss of electricity

Healing Light

The sun returns at daybreak
A pattern begins to form
Repetition of rethought
damages lower levels
of the heart structure

If I could take back
the stalwart opposition that marooned us
I would
in less than a fractured heart's beat

Bending through glass
Spreading across my eyes
This healing light
has a large task before it

Brook

The brook it flows
seething through grooves
discerning crevices
often meandering
always determined
finding its own course
Fluid in times of inelasticity
Enduringly relentless

My eyes follow
I want this as motto
To be this stream
driven yet guided
Let it take me
To be astonished
To know where it leads
To learn and discover just the same

Apparitions of Consequence

Fragile prints in clay
Broken days I can't have back
There's a piece of you in every memory

Impossibility of balance
between bridges of truth and acceptance
Amid the passage of dream and consciousness
you found me

No words with one million thoughts
I promised I'd always keep you safe
then I failed you

You made me whole
Now I'm half
Haunted by apparitions of consequence

Pictures are filaments of tribute
Proof of a work of genius
I am fortunate
to have shared this space with you

First Day

This is the first day
My historical viewing revives you
from a preconscious recollection
Empty melodies without chorus
Assemblies of stillness and silence
attempt to shift the balance

Imagery manipulation
A synopsis of your absence
A heart pulled down to a tomb
I refrain from thought fault lines
Reach for fallen trees in rapids of sadness

The proof of your sighting
represents ravines of reflection
I move into the sketch of the day
the first ordinary day without you

Modified Journey

A heliograph message is received
about a focus forcing shift
Cumulative texts to be rewritten
that will falsify my prophecy

Domain laws are no longer absolute
World view covenants are challenged
Unions of believers are disbanding
A missionary loses her mission
Nature loses species
Redirected to the unsurety of ways
in the narthex of our devotion

Congregants abandoned as palms raise
waiting for waterfalls to cleanse the sin
receiving incongruence as compensation
prognosticating an outer-darkness
where resolution must be discovered alone
with hope that everything isn't lost
This modified journey begins
significantly sooner than imagined

If I Live to See Tomorrow

An essential reunion
with timeless valley fires
bargaining with subzero skies
We are together but I'm alone

The day drew long
My patience stretched thin
My objective pushes me ahead
This insistence finds me unfound
Walls grow larger
Distance becomes greater
My feet are numbing
Hands are shaking
My beacon is fading
Who I am got the best of me
The best of me was you

Factions of fatigue invade my bones
Something pulls from the other side
The hand of a friend
or the ballad of death
There are only questions
How it ends
If I made amends
or amends made me

What I see in this corridor
if I have another breath
if I live to see tomorrow
it will be anybody's guess

Days Later

The seas rise with guilt
I'm lost in remnants of repentance
Broken upon by storms

Young stars fall
emptying the sky
leaving only the cold and dark
Can you see the earth lights where you landed?

There was so much to cultivate
though nothing would've changed
The artillery is dull
The orchestra is out of tune
In all of my born days
I never would've believed
in a tale such as this

Days later the expedition concludes
My part isn't over
until the numbers are up
until the mind accepts
what the heart cannot

The Water Comes to Meet You

We open the envelope together
Respecting his requests
We make acquaintance with his comrades

A week later we arrive
observing flags at half-mast
A bugler echoes in the distance
as we greet the deck officer

The tribute commences
Words are spoken in honor
A life of service
A sacrifice at sea
Tears are shed
The Chaplain reads from scripture
as prayers are said

Three rifle volleys
as the platform tilts
the casket drops
When the water comes to meet you
we'll know it's time to fade into the depths

The last sea anchor raises
Selfish pursuits are gone
Days and nights will be isolated
until we're friends with time again

Memories and Photographs

I wait for dawn
leave a note
make my way to the rooftop
prop the access door with a brick

Rain like scissors
The rubber surface slick
I reach the edge
look over the ledge
Signs along the parapet wall
camouflage my debate from the bustle below

I think I see heaven above
I reminisce on unanswered prayers
No declarations, R.S.V.P's, or excuses
So I'm told to take a leap of faith
I'm betting this isn't what they meant

Never could I have imagined this
Since you've gone there's no direction
I wonder what they could tell me
what solutions or alternatives
what certainty remains
when memories and photographs aren't enough?

Empty Chair

A cursory adaptation
stolen in chrome light
spotlights the empty chair
A dazzling display
as it dances through glass
in and out of clouds

A soul shrine
A daily tribute
Gratitude written upon the heart
A path by necessity
lost to necessary evils
Hoping you know forgiveness
It's all I could do

Time is a downpour
Weeks pass until courage materializes
During a reshuffling of minds and home
I rest in the empty chair
The traces of visions you left me
All of them still here
but right here I cannot stay
Your presence is strong in the air, in my heart
In my heart you will always be

Light On the Floor

The light on the floor
A feline's game to satisfy instinct
Chasing birds in shadows
inside a square playing field
donated by the window and the sun

The reoccurring sequence
Light shifting, shadows moving
He hunted them in open space
Waiting for returning light
He scheduled it into his busy day

One morning months later
I notice the light on the floor
It settles in his favorite place
My heart breaks with memories
I can't help but smile just the same
In the time he lived it made him happy
That was all that ever mattered to me

Zone of Exclusion

Our memories were muted
by intervals and requirement
Fear suppressed in our dreams
affecting conscious thought

During these long nights
my mind revisits in splinters
like scalpels penetrating skin

Our fear of reaction
greater than fear of discovery
or hope of recovery
Revisit the amusement park of horror
A memory we desperately want to forget

We eliminate that episode
like the tattered dolls we abandoned
Hold close our surviving loved ones
send apologies to future generations
who may not be so lucky

We are survivors
for better or worse
unclear if it's a blessing or curse
We attempt to smile a little every night
before we close our eyes

Seventeen Years

Often times I feared horizons
For seventeen years
I pivoted to the optimal view of the world
Seventeen years I was one way
certain of another year

Kings who ruled in harmony
now dredge the sand as servants
in a wasteland occupied by malevolence
with poverty in their thoughts

Historians sort through lost relics
discover sketches and stories
a unique snapshot in time
buried in musty periodicals
about a soul that defies imagination
and exceeds expectations

Ready for rediscovery
given to the universe as hope
too significant not to be resurrected
before a child's eyes
after she's been good all year

This spirit is shapeless and indestructible
summoned wherever there is peace
immune to effects of time and philosophy
There will never be an ending

I Remember

Empty docks starved for vessels
Discrete confusion on everyday faces
History gathers and stores the fantastical
Corpuscles stir in old blood
waiting for the approaching date

We believe everything in print
without challenge or question
Returning to the task at hand
Our words and actions at odds

Once upon a time we coexisted
like the sea and shore
We had unfinished business
after our voyage stalled in deep water

Stoned on significance
the fixation on changing the world
Sleeping through the years
when I could've saved you
had I cut through storms of misconception

I return to our shoreline
I don't recall who I was then
I find myself at your door
with an unfounded trust in modest concepts
I suppose my pieces have shattered
from my years away
I'd forgotten how to be extraordinary
to be necessary
but I do remember you

How Long

I waited
I was here when you wanted more
Thrilled when you found your anchor
I stood by when you pulled it up
as you signed the waivers to take on the sea

I roamed my thoughts, this countryside
deliberating for years
if you'd return for me
if you'd be the same

I endured
as your tour ended
your feet returned to land
I believed you when you said the day arrived
and you regained the ground you lost
but you're still searching
I'm still waiting
How long?

When you find your missing, broken pieces
I'll be the first and last to know
Until then...

Tide

Brigades of currents
Intrinsic swelling of the seas
My carrying guide
A participant, I call out
Inverse direction
to unknown territory
Unchartered lands
where I inhabit deserted islands
but always it calls
Always I return

The season becomes tiresome
My mind slides off track
over silicate minerals below
I fail to recall origins behind
A battle with sunsets ahead

Too fast, too soon
Gasping for air I fight the tide
Filamentous algae pulls me
I remain afloat to see the term

Remember me
It won't be long
before the tide carries on

Intersect

Accept this as my collective unconscious
You may begin to feel the same
in the after light

Never was I accused of caring too much
during the fabric of my initial defeat
Careful carelessness kept me callous
until I was starved for oxygen

Our hearts intersect for a moment
We call it life
A tale from two forelands

Our stories began alone
Begin again together

Life Flashes

In some waking dream state this morning
you left in the night
without warning or note
It carries enthusiasm and fear
like riding down a steep hill

I reflect on discourses
how much I know
pretend to know
say without thinking

A rich deviated misconception
as deep as the Congo River
high as the heavens some pray to
wide as the freedom you seek from yourself
hollow as the words we never said

We are nothing more than our actions
how we are to one another
Still I can't keep from throwing it away
when it matters most

In my life flashes
I see faces
connections I considered shallow
that might be as deep as the river
The unassigned significance was on my end
It was how I reacted
how I treated it
not the other way around

Broken Moon

I caught up with you
when you fell down from your peak
into your mountain valley
dealing with your own treason
disrupting your mind's sovereign state
insulting the broken moon
accusing it of failing you

You contest over bloodletting
letting it be, letting up
letting alone, letting it out
letting it go

Interference assaults presumptions
from a cultivated dialogue
that depicts you as articulated
without divulging your transparency

Now your mind is fasting
in its thirst for knowledge
Your currency an uninhibited retrovirus
filling institutions
since the earliest epoch of your age

Offering altered anger as equivalency
A trademark of ongoing oppression
It's all from your internal source
A directed response
as you seek to be committed and reordered
Just accept you're the catalyst
for this self-replicating rut
Don't blame the moon for your dark side

The Walk Alone

Surrounded by valley fields
I observe
My pace different when I walk alone
It strays from a fair-minded gait
I take time to look up
Sky blue and assorted shades
in a colored marker sky
obscures the tenure of desolate demons
now spineless and pale
from lack of neuromuscular activity
They lay motionless in the gulley
I refused an ear bending
to be comprehensively defeated
by their fading voices
They walked beside me one too many times

The interior of this composition
clockwork of my mind
So decorated and all for show
The fabric of my truth
originates from several tainted threads
It hypothesizes my receptive mood
until I reach the old town

I pass the man on the corner
with his English bulldog
We have the same conversation every time
I'm the only one who remembers

I find myself by the clay deposits
Melting glaciers refuse greenery and crops
The soil erosion has lessened the experience
The westerly fumes have changed my vision
lowered my essential values
diluting earthly purifications
from the weathered, faceless men

Still, there's a way around up ahead
The map shows no barriers
My appreciation prepares to lead the way
It's not the end of my road
nor the end of my days

Gift

My sense of sovereignty
contrary of youth and crisis
has been minute

If I had a vision of you
beyond my days
before my time
then everything would be certain

The everyday
A grenade in the mouth
when we never question
and do exactly as we're told

Wading into water
without any wake
Pleading for clairvoyance and miracles
We wait
Squandering any path to a higher place

Maybe the true gift
is each and every day
that we have breath
have life

These Hands

Maps of scars and salvation
or a telegraph of misappropriation
all over continents of mistakes

These hands
a transference
heritage
who I was or might be
A trace of my history
Encouraged
Magnanimous
Relinquishing my suppression of the light
Reaching through the dark
for your skin

I push ahead
until I see the turbulence of your silhouette
then fall back
in a game of trust
waiting to be collected
to be lifted
by your hands

For The First Time In A Long Time

The reign of storm clouds may be ending
These hands are open
feeling the last drops on my fingertips
We are still in the cold
I still don't know
For the first time in a long time
there are signs of hope

Have we convinced ourselves beyond logic?
Have we extrapolated all the undertones?
I thought of everything I know
to keep this rickety boat afloat
A wild fluttering bird afraid to land
A ship in hurricane winds lost at sea
It's time to come home
There's a story for you to complete

Fear strayed you far
Don't lose sight with one victory
You still have a long way to go
If this is your intent
then strap yourself in
There may still be sleeping giants ahead

Eyes forward
keep the entire frame in view
We'll fight the battles
alone and together
One day I hope we'll look back
and be glad we did

The Private Time After

Eyes from across the room
piercing holes
I don't know how to confront
There's a devil in the safe house
all over the details
He drops a bombshell
then falls back and behind
Conceals and codifies
as he breaks stale silence

Patience tumbles off the edge
into a tangle of passages
It leads to new elements
At the moment of no return
civilized thoughts emerge
A heated moment grows cold
Condemnation is detained
until the private time after

Until We Live

I feel ghosts in the walls
Shouting at movement
at all the injustice
He said it must hurt until we live

I set my standards low
held my head down
avoided eye contact
missed the jealous scenery

If I've been a substitute for joy
or a reason for desolation
then I've survived in spite of myself
and I'm here now
with stones as building blocks
On rubble I improve my vantage
I replace what's erased me
with mended thoughts
I build appreciation at storm fronts
for reasons I belong
I believe
It's not life until we live it

Adhesive

Through the Fresnel lens
The hierarchy of your choices diminish
A wealth of contradictions
A whetted blade cuts through mist and haze
into your nerves

Staggered to find you susceptible
before the summer chill
Your interests just an adhesive substance
Copied and collated

Ancient soul shaped images
ultimate origin unknown
sculpted to devote energy
to trivial matters
unaligned with your forces
Your plumage is unidentifiable
Your clay too absorbent

Discard your combative theories
Discover your fundamental doctrines
Contribute to the primary present
you unwittingly created

Before you lose the frequency
Before love and tolerance erodes
into the cracks you caused
Be advised there is no practice run
This is real and happening now

Rules

We leached under the tunnel
deviated through deserted streets
pried open the door and burned the books

I was never a big supporter
but they were convincing
with their emotional currency
We had to prove a point

Enough of the straight sides and angles
I couldn't be autonomous
with these restrictions

I anticipated
I was sure of the written policies
Certain I'd have time
that I'd have a reservation
Willing to put laughter on hold
Knowing there's a heaven
as long as I abide by the guidelines
Then why is the ground uneven?

I can't shake these electric jolts
It might be the memory of fun
playing by a different set of rules
or maybe it's the realization
that what I've sought isn't actually truth

Fortuneteller

We march through unsanctioned territories
Flames and soot overpower the sky
A darker blue still permeates
Old policies still resonate
Skeletons march to the frontline

You're not the only one to lose
I know you remember
I can't forget
Fortuneteller
you said you'd tell me how this ends

Minds have yet to be corrupted here
Time has yet to be hypothesized
The witnesses of truths before
are protests without words
They scour the land for resistance
now whispers among defeated winds
The hard way is now the easy way
reminiscing about simpler times
as the turn in shadows
is about to reveal our secrets

Hallucination without wires
In a partitioned sky I am alone
when I see an opening in the stars
I begin to plot my course
I close my eyes and free fall
For the moment I am indecipherable

Different Roads

We tried different roads along the way
The sirens still wail
The casket remains
I can't extend my arms
far enough to catch you
I chase dreams chasing me
I wake to a starved reality
Cold fingers on my spine
won't let up

I have to believe there's more below
where leaves are buried under the snow
a root system where a seed has fallen
after the foreshadowing autumn breeze

The motorcade takes its last route
The trail fades into the sunset
The town stalls for a moment
A new silence spreads over radio waves
and into our ears

These foreign sounds a heart must accept
The difference between the time we lost
and time we have left
Casual drifting along indifference
came at a cost

After one last look around
I close the door on dilapidated thoughts
toss the key into the nearby stream
appreciate the irony, the victory of defeat
never to return

What becomes of this area, this street?
Who will I be now?
It all remains to be seen

Conversation With A Ghost In A Bar

An afternoon memory
of cottages, small islands and Castlebay Harbor
reminded me I slept too long in your honor

I was passing by
when a voice in my head guided me in
I assumed that was you
The bartender was a young girl
she appeared to know her way around a bottle
doing acrobatic flips through catch phrases
keeping the saturated crowd on their toes
There were some crude comments of innuendo
about her evening plans
But often that's how it goes

She thought it strange
when I ordered a drink for two
"What's got you down?" she inquired
I said "I'm not the 'drown my sorrows' type."
"This one's for a friend."
She looked in your direction
I know she didn't believe me
but she said she saw you too

The first place I found you
is the last place I would've looked
I'm not sure why you're here
You haven't touched your glass
Our conversation stilted
My credibility wilted
So when the jester's pickup lines failed
and the circus monkey equivalents
turned their tricks for the crowd
When the witch cackles
like she outsmarted every fairy tale ending

I realized there are better ways
to converse with ghosts
At the door I remembered I forgot to tip
I returned to your empty glass
I'd like to think you got my money's worth
It was likely more tricks from the bartender
I'm satisfied without knowing for sure

Quiet Time

A short pause
A quiet time in morning
I wish it to stay
I hold an argument with the day
about the insistence to proceed
onto the importance of things
that aren't as important

In the end I always lose
accept defeat
If I keep trying
if I'm overly persistent
maybe one day I'll succeed

Winter's Tampering

I assume no shape or form
In this place of beautiful sunsets
I'm allowed to sleep when I should be awake
I've shed my bones and veins
I can acknowledge the absence of pain

Here all the strays have a bed
They forget their troubled past
Forgiven is the ignorance and neglect
Only gentle hands are familiar

My essence is a feather
drifting over burden and cold
settling in layers of peace and forgiveness
Here there is no now
Just a painting of my every memory

I know we couldn't prevent winter's tampering
For now we carry on apart
but you remain my radiant heat
in a sheath that keeps me

No complaints about your willed accommodations
cushions, catnip, scratching posts, and treats
a buffet with all one can eat

I conjured this dream session as a message
to assure you I've arrived
Here all love exists in its purest form
you can lift the anchors of your heavy heart

I will stall the impatient winds
await to resume our routine
until gravity sets you free
and determines it's your time to relocate

Seeds of Optimism

To the wraith in the corner
The summer wants to be dismissed
The cold wants in
The wind has died
around the windmills of regret
Seeds of optimism have broken
New life grows in their place
The old ways of this community
are malnourished and scattered
The festival of mourning was last month
So what's your objective for this obstinacy?
I can't help to think it's out of spite

Guilt is a demon feasting on pure souls
It doesn't hinder forward movement alone
Stop begging for more partisans
You've had your way
It's your turn to suffer
my turn to profit
by the income of enjoyment
I light a match to your cloak
I watch the last ashes of cloth oppression
float and swirl away in the air

Dear Ambivalence

What will she believe
when my mind is a mystery
my heart a memory?
If it stays this way
will she?
I fear what I'll become
if I let this run me

Dear Ambivalence
As the catalyst of self-fulfilling fear
you should shoulder some blame
You should be ashamed
for this stranglehold
in the fog you left

I need to change my rails
clear the ambiance
of dark reactions
to expect the outcomes I receive

Behind the curtain
it's always me pulling the strings
So here I am, dear ambivalence
I've decided I'm reversing roles
I'll be your wonder
your frustration and fear
I'll make you second guess me
as the waters run past you
Your experience dampened
by the internal thought of me
It's my turn to haunt you
as I live free

Shallow

I wade into water
to see the ocean floor beyond breakers
Often that is life
Shallow

I sat in session with shame
Through the heaviest of blizzards
to discover my theme music
my ambition
my calling

Then there's you
ostensibly so equipped
an outer shell so vibrant
Internal workings tell of upheavals

You've made the most of it
integrating puns of allegiance
My trepidation illuminates ciphers of jealousy
as I use you
my most unlikely source of stimulus
to rediscover my footpath

Circling a delinquent muse
drawing it back to fortitude
Giving credit where it's due
Abandoning the idea to blame you

Remembering a Friend

Owner of the sunlight
It approaches
I think of you today
Remembering caused a smile
Never did you bother me
while I stirred concoctions of misgivings
out in troubled bogs and marshlands
You left sculptures of variation
My shade of false light
could not contain your own tragedy
Recently my value increased
after the rainclouds found me
as they once did you

In the nighttime landscape of dreams we speak
all the ways we inferred
the volatile snapshots of our antiquity
Only now can I distinguish
the scars of your ten year war

If you need to face my direction
know I now understand what friends are here for
If you forgive my corroded past
we'll come out of it in time
preferably with time left
so I can be to you
the one you believed I was
the one you no longer need

Apology

For over a fourth-life
I believed my cause was just
I was bullet proof
trusting my trajectory
I thought mine was the only angle

I reached the rocky bottom
The fragility of moments were discovered
each smile
all promises
every heart

Burrowing in harsh climates
without delicate balance
Wasteful with feelings
I was hard on you
I lifted you when it served me
then fell apart
It was all I knew

I can't escape old dialects
It's nothing to you now
I was lost and found
I understand now

For all I never was
all I could've been
all you hoped I would be
my apology

Largest of Misconceptions

Deep in constellations
I imagine a blatant dissimilarity
where my zodiac reevaluates balance
I appropriate my capabilities
evaluate my culpabilities
assume relativity

If you're expecting acknowledgement
or remorse from reflection
you've crossed the wrong version of me

In consciousness of surroundings
lies the largest of misconceptions
By the time my waking state receives words
They've been shredded and reduced
to ruins of ineffectiveness

My clandestine pact
to the hero I lost
My shortcomings masquerade as assets
I avoid recognition
Stay this direction
for at least another year
I live in the prosaic valley
of the impression he left
I can let this go
I will

Surge Inside

Words collapse above me
I'm converted to resonance
Hollow from days afore
My skin is unresponsive

All my colors dye
blend into your background
meet you in camouflage
bleed down your walls
pool at your feet

Carrying hearts in a roundabout
Barely escaping trampling feet
Fearing next is last
This fear is greater than the final act

I sleep in thorns
petrified in position
Waiting on winter
to kill the intent of life
until I can move again
after brittleness thaws

Following frost
before growth
I barely open my eyes
when I see the sea come alive
I sense the surge inside
I know it's time to return, to arrive

The Day When Nothing Happens

The withdrawing concept draws your attention
settles down in your thoughts
We shout from cliffs by necessity
A whisper to observers below
Ambitions to cause avalanches
pass with rising light

There's so much space in a moment
hurling toward eternity
On a day like today
the nearness of you isn't far

Efficiency avoids chaos
Each side supports their cause
Sooner or later we all end here
These methods once avoiding us
begin to reveal themselves
We set out on an inward journey
When we stop looking
we find ourselves
on the day when nothing happens

One Of Those Stories

A steady keel
in a separate sea
Stars duel overhead
I've been here before
Some other lifetime

Comparable memories
Coordinates aren't the same
Mistakes that plagued me
just scars
lessons deep in tissue
from the times I didn't complain
didn't explain
before divide began

She said she remembered me
We found each other
We always will
I'm supposed to be astonished
It's supposed to be unfamiliar
Breaking new ground
Retracing my steps
I know the answer
I know what theory's proven next

This is my change order
I break the chain of hands
Night closes its window
Morning light on display
I'll always remember you fondly
but this is one of those stories
that has to end this way

One Eternal Moment

A blue jay calls
skies call back
His song falls to the ground
The sleeping world hums, stirs, and settles
then disappears
No sound of expansion
No hint of life
as if the problem of ourselves has been solved

I'm encouraged that I still hear the quiet
that it could last more than a minute
I accept what the great thinkers postulated
It's never too late to be more
I feel woven into weightlessness
for one eternal moment

Revelations In A Pub

An ambient southern pub
Rain drops quench the thirst of spring trees
I'm presented with an opportunity
to be tempted
A woman with a weight on her shoulders
carries a smile
Others they pass her by

As a younger man I'd have dreamt
of a scenario where I was worth her time
Today, nothing
What's more
this discovery was void of concern
I wondered why
Was I sad?
lost in self-pity?
dead inside?

These sessions of deductive reasoning
drew my conclusion
Despite all wrong turns and old disenchantment
no more crisis captures me
I've arrived
I am happy

Transparent Reflection

The final boarding call
delayed, midst and fog
Just a cyclical progression
I seek another rendition of myself

Sired in pity
Looking out over iridescent fields
Vacationing from words
Augured to comatose-like states

Unkempt
since I was caught in the act of caring
Mythological hypotheticals I worshipped
will be debunked by mid-afternoon

A transparent reflection
Observing flight preparations
mixed with dissecting glares
I unfix my stance
Shift with surges
Premonitions of destination dance in my head

I relocate my dominion
Target unified destiny
Elevated, conductive
I blend and inhabit
I think about the holiday season ahead
I get in line
This flight is a bridge between sentiments
It's all to find my way back to you

Core Sample

Green fields with wilted flowers
tilled for solutions
Nothing to nourish
I gravitated toward settled sand
where cracks in stone gave way
not fighting for their place
I dropped the load from my hands
the cargo from my stronghold

The core sample of my heart
revealed every known emotion
I recollected ineptness
until my vision altered
by her songs of the kaleidoscope

I waited a lifetime
Still unprepared for what was next
My belief in goodness and beauty
took physical form
With my next inhalation
everything had reason

Trespass

Mist glistens off the morning fields
Sun trespasses
affecting color
Bronzed hedges and crops surrender

Slowly climbing stockades
Edging in panes
where I want to be out
It slinks along walls
blinding like colorless pigment

It moves to the line
We are face to face
"Welcome" I say
"Please stay"

These Wings

The birds gather
begin their morning conversations
Their singing crescendos
They disperse like shrapnel into trees
at the sight of me
On branches they watch
I can feel them
With these wings I climb into the air
Fall and repeat
After several tries
I seem to have the technique

I am out over oceans
Waves deep
I see her in my dreams like memory
I soar by ghosts that have haunted me
Soon I'm in the clear and cleared to land
but I continue on
raising my altitude
I put distance behind me
between dark clouds and the horizon

It sounds trivial
but to me it's novel
I give back my fear
I feel nothing but pureness
I know great things are up ahead

Where I End

When she sees through fog
that I sought guidance through insults
knowledge with ignorance
then she knows

All the times I killed the conversation
rolled the eyes
walked away from uphill battles
forged the innocence of remembrance
took the light of those I loved

I traveled west
Stepped into new light
Made new promises
If I mourned the setting sun
I'd have to celebrate the rising
What goes down must come up
It will always rise

At the mountain foothills
by the last of the cottages
at the river's mouth
I watched families unite
Unfamiliar to me
not to them

Carousels of eyes
dancing in firelight
The turning phase of a forgotten smile
I knew I could begin here
This is where I end

www.ingramcontent.com/pod-product-compliance
Lightning Source LLC
Chambersburg PA
CBHW032058040426
42449CB00007B/1123